BIY

BODGE IT YOURSELF

BIY

BODGE IT YOURSELF

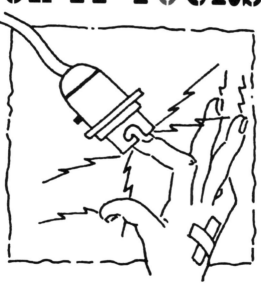

Why pay someone to wreck your home?

David Jacobson · Jess McAree

ABOUT THE AUTHORS

David Jacobson is a journalist who has worked for national magazines and radio stations. He lives in Surbiton, the 'BIY Bible Belt', and is a life-long Bodger himself.

His major achievements include nailing his hand to a picture rail; slipping on wallpaper paste and hurtling through a window; and destroying a £5,000 Persian rug while attempting to drain a radiator.

He has made so many visits to his local DIY superstore that he claims to know not only every tune played on the in-store muzak system but also the order in which they come.

Jess McAree is also a journalist who works on magazines and national newspapers. He is co-author of 'Mischief and Delight', an anthology of poetry about kittens.

His lamentable attempts at homemaking are a byword for ineptitude amongst his peers. Listing shelves, patchy paintwork and an exploding boiler make his south London home a monument to BIY.

He estimates that his spending on home improvements must by now equal the municipal dept of a small third world city. Yet his flat still looks like one.

ACKNOWLEDGMENTS

Sincere thanks is extended to Derek Gilchrist, Claire Sefton, Jess's aunt Celia and Dave's mum Rachel for inspiration; Maggie Underwood and Chris Dart for their artistic endeavours; Cüneyt Kizilelma and Susan Williams for technical support (they lent us their computer); Tony and Maureen Nakhimoff for knitting tips; and Lennart Sjöstrom and James Potter (GCSE French Grade G) for their invaluable (and cheap) translation services.

Especial thanks to Charles for actually believing this was a good idea. There's one born every minute.

First published in 1995 by

Two Heads Publishing
9 Whitehall Park
London
N19 3TS

ISBN   1-897850-06-9

Book & cover design by Mick McCarthy and Mical Yeowell
Illustrations by Chris Wilson
Printed & bound by Caldra House Ltd., Hove, Sussex

CONTENTS

INTRODUCTION 3

1: SAFETY IN THE WORKPLACE . . .5

2: GETTING STARTED 10

3: HOME DECORATING 14

4: ELECTRICS 24

5: PLUMBING 32

6: HOME SECURITY 40

7: FIXTURES AND FITTINGS 45

8: EXTERIOR WORK 51

9: BIY PROJECTS 57

INTRODUCTION

Over the past decade bodging has become the nation's favourite pastime. Once the preserve of a few select artisans who charged a fortune to wreck our homes for us, we now have the wherewithal to bodge it ourselves, cheaply, easily and with aplomb.

This book is aimed at both the aspiring handyman with limited knowledge of bodging and the habitual Bodger.

Compiled with the aid of hundreds of experts from around the world† it distils, for perhaps the very first time, literally a lifetime of hints, tips and techniques in one handy, compact volume.

Through a series of computer-enhanced diagrams and cheery, friendly text you'll find sections on all aspects of bodging — from recommended ways of electrocuting yourself and your entire family to putting up listing shelves; from coping with a Boeing 747 wedged in your roof to building a family crypt.

So roll up those sleeves, get out that toolbox and start Bodging It Yourself. With our help and advice your home will soon become a brighter, happier and altogether more interesting place in which to live.

† AUTHORS' NOTE
Although the information in this book has been meticulously checked and double checked for complete and utter accuracy, errors of a minor nature can creep in. The authors therefore cannot accept any responsibility for electrocution, drowning, poisoning, gassing, strangulation, cardiac arrest, radiation sickness, spontaneous combustion or general mutilation which may arise from anyone following the advice contained herein.

FURTHER NOTE
The authors also wish to make it clear that no animals were in any way harmed or mistreated during the research for this book. All pets led long and useful lives and were subject to proper and decent burials.

1
SAFETY IN THE WORKPLACE

A BIYer's prime concern must always be the safety of himself and those around him. Remember, a careless mishap and you could spend three months trussed up on a traction couch in your local hospital. There you could be neglected by NHS nurses working out their notice before they leave for private practice, and injected daily with the wrong drugs by overworked junior doctors on their last legs from a 72-hour shift. And that's if you don't die of Legionnaire's Disease first.

So, to avoid this unhappy fate, always remember the simple acronym:

Be safe

Or face

The possibility of ending up on

Crutches or even in

Hospital

SAFETY IN THE WORKPLACE

Can you spot the common safety error?

Well, did you spot it? Yes, that's right. The window should always be kept open to allow for ventilation.

LADDERS

All ladders are potentially hazardous. Check for missing or extra rungs. Take nothing for granted. Trust nobody.

It's vital to check for woodworm, too. You might like to enlist the help of an elderly or annoying neighbour to test your ladder first.

CHEMICALS

Chemicals, like dentists, must always be treated with respect and held at arm's length. Don't be tempted to save storage space by mixing all your chemicals in one container or a chemical reaction might occur.

Never mix your chemicals

Instead, keep chemicals in an orderly, user-friendly 'library' by employing the simple Von Blücher symbol system (shown right) pioneered by the eponymous German scientist and war criminal.

TESTING CHEMICALS

Every BIYer will, at one time or another, come across an unlabelled jar containing a 'mystery' chemical substance. Using the storage system outlined above should prevent this, but if it does occur employ the following simple tests to determine the chemical's identity.

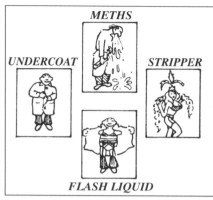

The Von Blücher symbols

How to determine the identity of a mystery chemical substance

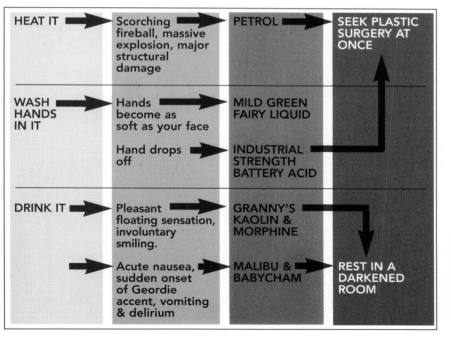

HEAT IT →	Scorching fireball, massive explosion, major structural damage →	PETROL →	SEEK PLASTIC SURGERY AT ONCE
WASH HANDS IN IT →	Hands become as soft as your face →	MILD GREEN FAIRY LIQUID	
	Hand drops off →	INDUSTRIAL STRENGTH BATTERY ACID	
DRINK IT →	Pleasant floating sensation, involuntary smiling. →	GRANNY'S KAOLIN & MORPHINE	
→	Acute nausea, sudden onset of Geordie accent, vomiting & delirium →	MALIBU & BABYCHAM →	REST IN A DARKENED ROOM

GLUE

Take care when using glue. Something as innocent as a tube of household adhesive can turn into a monstrously lethal weapon in the wrong hands.

Always use glue in a well-ventilated room. If you breathe in fumes the following may occur:

1. Dizziness followed by
2. Short term memory loss and
3. Convulsions with
4. Psychosexual trauma leading to a
5. Complete neural shutdown and finally
6. Total insanity

FIRE

Fire is no laughing matter. A small blaze can sweep through the average house in minutes, destroying everything you hold dear. It is no respecter of age, sex or class. It

knows no geographical boundaries.

For example, in a recent case, a cigarette left carelessly burning on a sofa owned by Lord Baggleswick of Rothshields resulted in a major conflagration, destroying not only his beautiful 17th century country seat, but also four warehouses, three factories and a used car lot six miles away. Fortunately Lord Baggleswick had the foresight to take out an insurance policy on the morning before the incident and was thus able to purchase a small Caribbean island with his £6.5 million payout. But you may not be so lucky.

It therefore makes sense to always follow the BIY Fire Code:

- **Install firemen's poles throughout the house**

- **Affix a rope ladder to the attic window leading down to the front lawn (you can easily knit one using our pattern)**

- **Wear asbestos pyjamas**

As an added precaution, it is wise to make a safety announcement whenever a guest arrives. We would suggest something along the following lines:

Good morning.
On behalf of Ernie and Betty Bagshaw welcome to 45 Acacia Gardens, Rottingdean. In the unlikely event of a major inferno ripping through the lounge and igniting the cheap acrylic cushion covers, you will find an old fire blanket located in the airing cupboard just underneath Ernie's underwear (point vaguely in direction of hall). We hope you enjoy your visit and look forward to seeing you again.'

To knit a rope ladder

You will need:
- *12 x 50g balls of Beehive Shetland Floss (black)*
- *No 11 (3mm) needles*

With bk cast on 25 sts and ss 6 rows. Inc 1 st at each end of next row — 37 sts. Ss 4 rows. Repeat last 6 rows, twice more — 42sts. Ss 148 rows. *
*** P1 row. Dec 1 st at beginning of next 2 rows. Break yarn and leave sts on a st holder.

FLOODS

A flood is probably the most distressing of all natural disasters. As rivers begin to rise and tropical storms lash northern latitudes due to global warming, the likelihood increases that one day your belongings will, literally, float out of the window.

The judicious placing of sand bags at key points around your home may help, as would the use of a small syphon pump. However the only foolproof way of dealing with a catastrophe of this nature is to build an ark.

To build an ark

You will need:
- *200 felled Canadian spruces*
- *10,000 x 4½ inch nails*
- *Several rolls of strong twine*
- *2 aardvarks... 2 zebra*

As soon as your ark is constructed, simply round up a male and female representative of every species on earth. Your local pet supplier should be able to help you. You will need someone to feed — or feed to — the animals. You may like to ask your neighbour. In general however, you will find that your ark will be low maintenance as most of the animals will end up eating each other.

Some common safety queries

Q. After a percussive bell ringing accident, I was left with just one leg. Obviously I find it difficult to climb a ladder safely. Can you offer any advice? (DM, Swansea)

A. Why not make yourself a wooden limb? See our accompanying volume: The BIY Guide to Making Prostheses on a Shoestring.

Q. While reaching up to paint the picture rail in my living room I accidentally slipped into my grand piano and am now hopelessly entangled in the strings. My left leg is trapped under the bottom C hammer and my chin is precariously wedged in the lid support. Any moment now my 7-year-old son Norman will be returning home to practise his scales. Help! What can I do? (DG, Hampton Wick)

A. Reach out with your right hand to the piano stool and extract the score to Chariots of Fire by Vangelis. Hopefully, if Norman plays it, the continued repetition of the base D flat will free your leg. On the other hand, if he chooses to play, say, the first movement to Grieg's Piano Concerto, you really will have a problem.

2
GETTING STARTED

So let's take it from the top...

CHOOSING THE AREA

Estate agents will tell you that three things matter when choosing a property: Location, location and location. Although this is generally sound advice, do not rule out properties in apparently undesirable areas. Not only are such homes cheap, they also offer hidden advantages.

For instance, the inconvenience of living next to a major international airport may at first seem considerable. But at slack moments in the landing and take-off schedule, you and your guests will benefit from unrivalled free parking on the runways.

CHOOSING THE PROPERTY

It is all too easy to be seduced by the breathy prose of your fawning estate agent's literature, and to be lulled into complacency by the airy confidence of a ludicrously over-qualified surveyor. He almost

Some snags a surveyor might m

No roo

Yogic flying club of Great Britain

Proposed route of n
12-lane M400 superhig

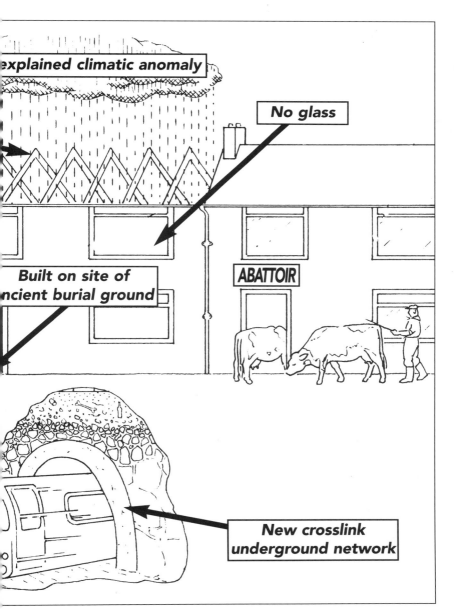

Always check behind the scenes

certainly surveyed your home through a pair of binoculars from a window seat in the Coach and Horses down the road.

What's more, the most diligent local authority search can also miss the odd little fault that may cause the occasional problem for the amateur BIYer in years to come. So always be on your guard.

It's also wise never to take anything at face value. Always check behind the scenes to make sure you are getting what you paid for.

SETTING FOOT IN A DIY STORE

Having acquired your home you will want to get cracking on BIY. Once upon a time, you would have faced days of toil just assembling the materials required. Trips would have

had to be made to the timber yard for wood, the hardware store for nails, the plumber's merchant for pipes and fittings.

Today, thankfully, it's all a lot easier. One quick — and pleasurable — trip to your nearest *Bodge It All* will provide everything you need.

Of course, it's just possible that you've never visited a superstore before. If so, here's a quick guide to the treats that lie in wait...

Having parked in the completely empty car park on the Bexleyheath Gas Works Light Industrial Trading Estate, you will step through the doors of an outsized tin shed, straight into a world of wonder. Indeed, as you amble down the deserted aisles you may start to wonder how a 3,500 sq metre building can be staffed by just one spotty adolescent called Darren and a hapless checkout girl with the IQ of a plank of chipboard.

This is because in their tireless quest for economy, the Management have ruthlessly cut unnecessary overheads (like staff) to pass on savings to you, the Customer. Fortunately you will not need to ask anyone for help, since just about everything is clearly labelled 'easy-to-assemble' and 'no special tools required.' In the unlikely event that you should want to check some trivial point, Darren in the smart poly-cotton boiler suit will effortlessly dazzle you with his brilliant grasp of BIY methods and techniques.

Should you have some particularly esoteric query beyond Darren's ken, you will be forced to kidnap the manager, chain him to a radiator (you'll find these in the aisle marked 'Plumbing') and hold him hostage until somebody, anybody, explains to you why they only sell 1 ¼ inch woodscrews in multipacks of 2,000. You will locate the manager in the office marked 'Manager'. He will be the one slumped over a copy of *What*

Woodwork?, surrounded by unopened boxes of turpentine and white spirit, with a fag in his mouth, sprinkling ash onto the poorly-laid brown tweed carpet tiles.

Once you've loaded your trolley with shop-soiled end-of-line bargains you need simply wheel it over to the checkout where the gawping assistant will entertain you as she bounces up and down on a pogo stick trying to scan the bar code on the end of a 12ft RSJ.

TOOLS OF THE TRADE

The novice BIYer will no doubt be tempted to splash out on a vast array of expensive tools such as claw hammers, pliers, saws, screwdrivers and chisels. This, as any old hand will tell you, is a futile waste of money. Nearly all jobs can be tackled with one handy, all-purpose tool: the pneumatic drill.

Highly valued by crazed psychopaths and Camden Council's Highway Planning Department for the maximum disruption, irritation and offence that it provokes, this versatile tool will rip through the toughest of tasks (and nerves) in a trice.

From hanging pictures to bashing up a quick ornamental rockery, the pneumatic drill's unique capabilities are well worth every penny of its £5,000 price tag.

How to spot a manager

BODGE SPLODGE
Sex life in the doldrums? A pneumatic drill also makes one hell of a sex aid. Doubles as an emergency electric toothbrush, too

3
HOME DECORATING

PAINTING

Much has been written about the importance of preparation when it comes to painting. Traditional DIY manuals spend pages emphasising the need for rubbing down woodwork, sugar-soaping walls and applying copious quantities of undercoat. Obviously it cannot be said too often that this is all a tedious waste of time and the competent BIYer need not concern himself with it.

The golden rule of painting is simple: Slap It On Quick

To start decorating, take the lid off the pot of paint. This enormously facilitates removal of its contents. Covering up furniture, removing pictures and taking down curtains is superfluous — just paint around them. Any splashes of paint will simply create a pleasing co-ordinated effect.

Applying paint

In the past, people painted with a brush and put up with huge streak marks where their over-applied

To paint a room

You will need:
• A pot of paint
• A brush
• A room

Types of paint available

• Gloss — gives an easy-wipe surface ideal for bulimics and sufferers of projectile incontinence
• Matt — for painting mats
• Undercoat — for painting under coats
• Masonry paint — for painting masons

dollops of paint ran down the walls. Luckily, they didn't have to endure them long, since they all died at 35 from the noxious lead and arsenic used in their paint and wallpaper.

Still, with today's emphasis on unusual and subtle painting effects, the BIYer has greater leeway in covering up careless errors. That great dribble of paint over the fireplace, for example, can now be passed off as an old Etruscan marbling effect. And that unsightly damp patch that no amount of paint will disguise is magically transformed into pre-distressed, post-modernist ageing.

Brushes

If you do not have a brush, don't worry. Many professionals achieve stunning results using everyday household items. Here are a few tricks of the trade:

- A Brillo pad or stale Shredded Wheat gives a delightful 'rustic' look to walls and ceilings

- Any old nappies lying around the house? Dipped in paint they can be recycled into paint pads

- A recently deceased small domestic pet makes the perfect rag-rolling tool

How much paint will I require?

Fill a measuring jug with water. Now 'paint' the walls with it. See how much you've used and then buy the equivalent quantity in paint.

As a general rule however, just follow these guidelines:

- Large areas: Quite a lot
- Medium areas: Average amount
- Small areas: Just a little

Stripping old paint

If you really have nothing better to do than to strip woodwork, there are several ways to do it:

- Chemical strippers — household brands do an excellent job but can be expensive
- Hot air gun (see below)
- Dynamite — an extremely effective and rapid method of paint removal, obtainable from your local munitions supplier. Charges should be affixed and primed with a proprietary detonator. A connecting cable should then be run at least 25 yards away

WARNING: *As with all household high explosives, care should be taken to follow the manufacturer's instructions*

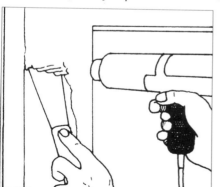

Correct way to use hot air gun

Incorrect way to use hot air gun

Painting doors

Doors, particularly your front door, are the most important thing you ever paint. Visitors will spend time examining them while waiting for you to answer the doorbell. So, calculate the average height of your friends and relatives and then paint a perfect two-inch band across the door at mean eye level. To be politically correct, paint another band lower down for the vertically challenged. The rest of the door can be ignored.

Note: If you do not like panelled doors, keep applying layers of paint to the sunken panels until they become flush with the rest of the door.

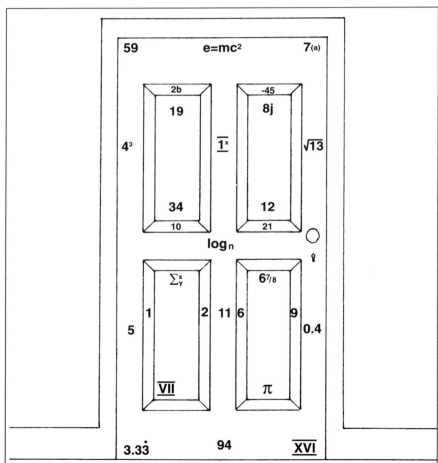

When painting doors always paint in order of numbers

Exterior painting

Although at first sight it may seem time-consuming and expensive, glossing the entire exterior of your house will handsomely repay you in years to come. Applying several thick coats to its brickwork and roof will create a tough, waterproof seal resisting the ravages of the British climate. It will also make your house stand out.

Order of painting

Always start from top left side of ceiling. Circumnavigating the ceiling rose, descend on bottom right corner of skirting, thence rising to top of door architrave opposite rear back wall, plunging towards middle of window wall dado rail.

Also, always work from right to left. Unless you're left handed. In which case, don't.

Beware of painting floors. It's easy to get carried away and paint yourself into a corner. If you do find yourself marooned at room's length away from the door, don't panic. With a 60 ft length of pre-tensioned high-tensile steel rope, a reinforced falconer's gauntlet, two pulleys and a little

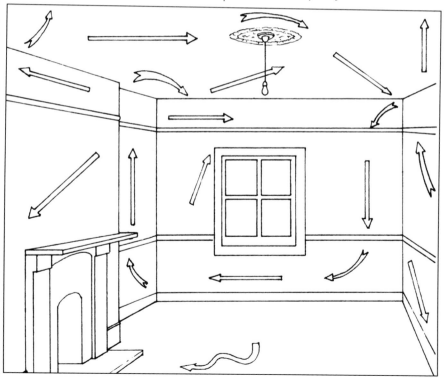

Stick to this plan and painting couldn't be easier

positive thinking you should be able to winch yourself to safety.

Textured paints

Creating traditional swirls and fan patterns with textured paints is easy but dull. Be brave. Break out and try something a little more imaginative: For that 'Hollywood' look get your family and friends to make palm prints up and down your walls. Alternatively, bottom prints make a risqué talking point.

The importance of colour

The first step to successful painting is choosing the right colour. Leaflets from paint manufacturers present a bewildering pallet of exotically

Colours come in all shades and hues

named colours — from Nipple Pink and Gan Green to Bidet Brown.

In general, light colours such as white or beige create a feeling of spaciousness and harmony.

Conversely, darker colours, such as black, tend to induce a sense of hopelessness and despair which may ultimately lead to suicide.

If in any doubt always plump for light green. A firm favourite in DSS offices and sanatoria, its effect is the BIY equivalent of a full-frontal lobotomy. Or watching eight hours of daytime TV. Especially Richard and Judy.

WALLPAPERING

Given the time, effort and expense of wallpapering your home compared to slapping up a bit of paint, it's truly astounding that anyone actually bothers. Still, if you must...

To paper a room

You will need:
* *Wallpaper*
* *Something to stick it up with*
* *A wall*

To start

1. *Unroll a suitable length of paper*
2. *Moisten with paste*
3. *Apply to wall*
4. *Repeat till wall is covered*

Experts commonly agree that it helps to match wallpaper patterns correctly.

Remember to stop when you have papered the whole room. Unlike paint, wallpaper rarely needs a second coat.

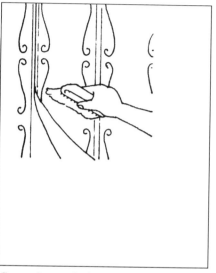

Correctly matched pattern

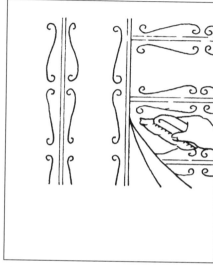

Incorrectly matched pattern

Different types of wallcovering

There are many types of wallpaper available. And many that aren't... but perhaps ought to be. If you have strong views on this issue, why not drop a line to your MP?

Common types include:

● Anaglypta — named after Mme Anna Glypta, the infamous 16th century French brothel proprietress

● Florals — for a soft and feminine look. Like a cheap French knocking shop

● Scarlet flocks — to give the imitable ambience of your local Tandoori take-away. Or a Bombay bordello

BODGE SPLODGE

If you're thinking of buying woodchip paper, don't bother. A similarly interesting dimpled effect can be obtained much cheaper by repeatedly firing a 12 bore shotgun at the wall

Trick of the trade

If strips of paper fail to meet, gaps between them can be cunningly disguised by carefully copying the design onto the wall with a felt marker pen. From the right distance and in the right light, no one will ever notice.

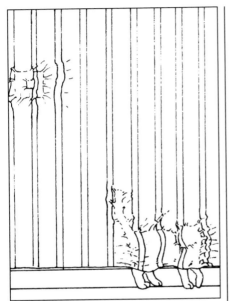

Spot the mistake?

Papering a ceiling

Tough one this. Don't bother even trying. Instead, why not consider the following:

- For a 'Polynesian village' look, weave pampas grass over a lattice of bamboo poles. Attach to ceiling with a spot of Uhu

- For an Igloo effect, use ice cubes from the freezer to 'tile' your ceiling in neat rows using a proprietary all-weather adhesive. Note: this is only advisable for those dwellings situated in polar latitudes

- Ceiling paintings. Since ancient times man has strived to decorate his home with artistic outpourings. There is no reason why you, too, should not adorn your ceiling with beautiful biblical scenes

Some common wallpapering queries

Q. *I live in a lighthouse off the North Orkneys and am having difficulty papering my lounge, a cylindrical stone room 8 feet wide and 120 feet high. Any ideas? ('Portland' Bill, North Sea)*

A. Yes. Simply affix velcro pads at 4ft intervals up the wall. Now abseil down the room attaching wallpaper as you descend. Incidentally, the velcro will also enable you to save your wallpaper from floods at high tides.

Q. *As an internationally renowned author with a fatwah on my head I don't manage to get out quite as often as I would like. Consequently I am getting rather tired of looking at the wallpaper. What would be your advice? (SR — name and address withheld)*

A. For that 'literary look', paste up pages torn from any remaindered novels you may have lying around. Or, should you have a biblical bent, tear out the pages from old religious texts.

TILING

Tiles, like condoms, come in many shapes, flavours and colours. Ceramics are ideal where a hard-wearing and waterproof surface is essential eg in a bathroom, shower cubicle, urinal, mortuary etc.

To tile a room

You will need:
• *Tiles*
• *Adhesive*
• *Somewhere to stick them*

How many tiles will I need?

Few things are more frustrating than arriving home from the tile shop only to find that you have insufficient tiles to complete your task. So follow this simple formula to ensure you buy the correct number:

$$T = \text{sq of } \frac{S \times W^3 \text{ divided by } \pi}{Z \times F}$$

where:

T = no of tiles required

S = width of wall

W = length of wall

Z = colour of tile

F = distance to the tile shop

How to stick up tiles

1. Using a cartographer's theodolite, measure the elevation of your room and the angles subtending from the top corners to the centre. With a sextant, calculate the mean latitudinal position of the proposed uppermost tier of tiles and align on a north-south polar axis. Then...
2. Stick tiles to wall

Cutting tiles

Don't be fooled! There is only one way to cut ceramic tiles – with an industrial diamond-tipped rotary saw.

TROUBLESHOOTING GUIDE

Problem: *My tiles keep falling off the wall*

Solution: *Stick them back*

Problem: *My tiles keep cracking as I attach them to the wall*

Solution: *You are nailing the tiles to the wall. Try glue*

Problem: *I have ended up with a matt brown wall surface covered in curious grooves and the repeated legend 'Made in Bulgaria'*

Solution: *You have stuck up your tiles back to front. The shiny surface should always face outwards*

Other types of tile

● Cork — insulates against cold and noise. Ideal if you live next door to an Icelandic heavy rock band

● Carpet tiles — can be made by purchasing a new carpet and cutting into neat 12 inch squares

Dirty carpets? Sprinkle some Scott's Porridge Oats on the floor. Much cheaper than Shake 'n' Vac and just as effective

THOSE FINISHING TOUCHES

By now, you will have a professionally decorated blank canvas on which to stamp your own individual artistry and imagination. But however grand the broad sweep, those little finishing touches are all. Imagine St Paul's without its dome. The Statue of Liberty without its torch. Blackpool Tower without Blackpool.

Stenciling

Why stick to stencilling flowers and geometric shapes. Be bold. Try:

● Organs of the body

● Autographs of your favourite celebs

● Surgical implements

● Islands of the South Pacific

Pictures

If you get easily bored with framed pictures you might like to consider making a display, similar to those motorised 'rolling' advertisements you see on the side of bus shelters. To do this is easy. Take a large Venetian blind and two contrasting prints. A copy of Botticelli's Birth of Venus and a picture of Samantha Fox would be ideal. Now put both prints through an industrial shredder and re-assemble, sticking

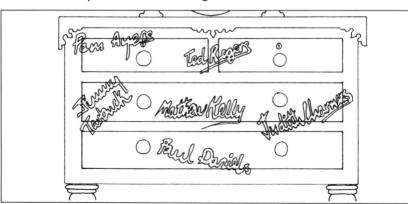

Unusual stencils make a good talking point

strips of each picture onto corresponding sides of the blind. You will now have a display that can be changed to suit your mood.

Disguising blemishes

Should any really nasty cracks appear in your plasterwork as you hammer in nails, you can always turn them into murals of trees using a coloured felt pen.

In the event that you puncture a main pipe, sending a torrent of water gushing into the living room, this can be disguised as a charming mural of a great African waterfall.

Plants

No home is complete without some greenery. So:

● For an instant arboreal effect, grow trees by digging through the foundations and planting directly in the soil beneath

● To recreate a tropical rainforest employ sprinklers in the ceiling, heat to maximum and cover windows with black bin liners. Purchasing poisonous spiders and snakes from your pet supplier will add a truly authentic feel

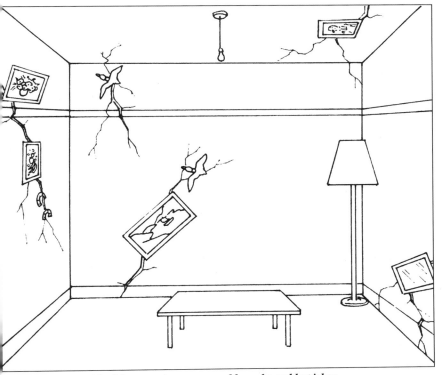

Wallhangings are ideal for covering up any odd marks or blemishes

4
ELECTRICS

Many people are scared of tackling electrical work for fear of 240 volts of raw power surging through their body turning them into a char-grilled doner kebab. This is highly irrational. Electrical work is perhaps the easiest and most satisfying task a BIYer can undertake. Any fool can rewire a house for next to nothing without the slightest risk of any personal injury whatsoever.

COPING WITH A CARDIAC ARREST

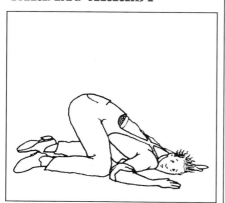

The recovery position

1. Keep as calm as possible as the victim starts to sizzle in a haze of acrid blue smoke

2. Using a long non-conductive pole eg punt pole, window pole, telegraph pole (disconnected) prod the victim away from the power source.

3. Now arrange him in the recovery position illustrated. You might like to offer words of comfort such as: 'You know, that new frizzy hairstyle really suits you' or 'Don't worry. The ambulance should be here any day now.'

4. Photograph the victim writhing on the floor for insurance purposes. In the event of a query it would be a shame to lose out on any payments you might be entitled to.

To attempt electrical work

You will need:
- *A length of wire*
- *A small screwdriver*
- *A full-sized rubber body suit*
- *A comprehensive all-risks insurance policy*

Most manuals recommend turning off the power at the mains before attempting any work. The BIYer, though, will obviously regard this as foolish advice. After all, how can you possibly work in the evening if the lights are off? And how can you run all those essential labour-saving power tools?

INSULATION

To be doubly sure of complete safety it is important to insulate the body from top to toe in rubber. Make your own protective suit by cutting up old car tyres and sewing them together with fishing line. You now have a made-to-measure hi-voltage tuxedo.

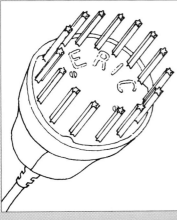

How to wire a plug

British plugs come with three terminals — earth, live and neutral — each corresponding to a different coloured wire.

Wiring a plug is elementary provided you remember which colour is which. To avoid confusion we offer this simple colour association aide-memoire:

BLUE = colour of sea = first letter of cuckoo clock = made in Switzerland = NEUTRAL

STRIPED = zebra = aardvark (fellow inhabitant of Africa) = AAAAA Acme Cabs = 'Ere, do you know who I had in the back of my cab once? That big geezer what was in the Terminator...' = Planet Hollywood = EARTH

BROWN = sounds like Eva Braun = Hitler's girlfriend = evil = anagram of LIVE

From midnight December 31, 1999, it is rumoured that Brussels will be introducing the European Regulatory Inter-Connector. This new plug, or ERIC as it will be known, will have not three but 15 terminals, one for each member state of the federation. After the millennium, every electrical appliance from a sandwich toaster to a Parisian pooper-scooper will have a 15-core wire. For simplicity's sake, wires will be coded in the colours of member nations' flags. However, there are several points to note:
● On no account should the German wire be connected to a sunbed
● In accordance with strict French linguistic pollution legislation, the ERIC will be known in France as the JEAN-JACQUES
● A 16th, Swiss wire may be introduced later. This will be gold-plated and fully insulated to keep it away from other pins

A design fault in prototypes led to the British wire frequently melting and disabling the ERIC. This was resolved by bypassing it totally, thereby rendering it a purely cosmetic feature that will play no part in the working of the plug.

Ask the experts

We have here enlisted the help of some old hands in the electrical business to answer your most common queries:

Q. *A few minutes ago, while wiring up an Acme 'Ring-a-Ling-a-Ding' melody doorbell in my sauna, I inadvertently stuck my big toe in the steam brazier and wired myself into the circuit. A frenzied, heavy metal 'Greensleeves' is now blasting out of the chime box whilst I am fried by 240 volts. What should I do?*
(CF, Haywards Heath)
A. It depends upon the make of your sauna. Many Swedish brands, such as the excellent SvenSmeg SwetuKlene 2000, benefit from an emergency power breaker which will doubtless cut in any moment and save your life (if not, SvenSmeg promises a full refund to dead or otherwise dissatisfied customers). On the other hand, if yours is a cheap, popular Czech sauna — the Chernobyl Skodasteam, for instance (£21.99, plutonium not included) — you are almost certainly doomed to a lingering, painful death.
(Sven Smeg, Manager, SvenSmeg Saunas, Oslo)

Q. *I am shocked. I have just received an electricity bill for £1,586 for the last quarter. How can I save on power in the future?*
(SG, South Norwood)
A. Try wiring your home's power sockets in series, rather than in parallel. Appliances plugged into the last few sockets on the circuit may function rather poorly — bread in your toaster, for instance, may take twice as long to brown (we find it helpful to have an expert standing by to check when it's ready) — but this is a negligible price to pay for considerable power savings.
(S Petrovani, Governor, San Quentin Penitentiary, Ca, USA)

Q. *How can I be sure the light is not still on when I close the fridge door?*
(PJ, Teddington)
A. Tenez! Voilà l'un des plus vieux problèmes qui aient jamais troublé la philosophie. Le seul moyen de le résoudre, c'est d'enfoncer un petit garçon dans le frigot et le laisser y passer la nuit. Ensuite, le matin, entraînez-le dans votre lit pour bien l'interroger sur l'éclairage de l'ampoule, tout en lui caressant les membres avec les votres....
(A. Gide, Philosopher, Paris, France)

A. Listen... er... it's a problem... an old problem... that never... sorry, always... troubled philosophers. The only... um... resolution is to... er... something about a little boy... in a fridge... at night. Then in the morning... er... in your bed... interrogate his pyjamas... is that right?...by the armpits... caressing the members of his family... with a vulture...
(Translation supplied free by James Potter, aged 14, GCSE Grade G)

Q. *I am currently involved in a project concerning the re-animation of human tissue by use of natural electricity. Where can I obtain some lifeless matter on which to continue my experiments?*
(Baron Von F, Liechtenstein)
A. Shergar can be found at the Sniff-U-Like Glue Company, Ballymeena, Co Antrim
(K D O'Leary, author: 'Shergar: Where Is He Now?')

ELECTRICS

CUTTING DOWN ON YOUR ELECTRICITY BILLS

What with the imposition of VAT on domestic electricity and the ever-increasing greed of the electricity boards, it makes sense to look at ways of cutting down on your consumption of power.

To get some idea of how this could be achieved, let's look at a typical couple (below) to see where they expend power and how they could make savings.

The use of small children

Do you have a young child who has a paper round or Saturday job? Then convince them that your coin-operated electricity meter is actually a money box. This will instil a strong sense of moral responsibility in them. It will also pay for your quarterly electricity bill.

Tapping into an electricity sub-station

Do you live near a sub-station? Then why not take advantage of the potential for free power?

Although sub-stations carry earnest signs warning of the dangers of several million volts lurking within, these notices are simply designed to frighten off people who, unlike yourself, have no knowledge of electricity whatsoever.

To get started run a cable from your fuse box across the street to the sub-station. Now simply connect your wire to the main switch. This will be the one marked On/Off.

Camouflaging the trailing cable with painted road markings is recommended in order to hide it from any authority who may wish to sue you.

Case study

Martin and Sarah live in a leafy London suburb. Martin, a junior writer for a little-known gardening magazine, usually takes a quick shower before work while Sarah makes the breakfast. This expends a total of 6 units of electricity: 2 on the electric shower, 1 on an electric kettle and 3 on a toaster used to make Martin's Marmite soldiers.

During the morning Sarah hosts Ann Summers parties. This uses up 2,454 units on powering assorted electrical appliances. Later, while she's out, Martin pops home with his friend Darren for steamy sessions in their Whirlpool bath (668 units). In the evening Martin works out on his electric Bullworker (42 units) before cleaning his teeth (1 unit) and switching out the light (0 units).

So, how could the couple save energy?

Well, Sarah could cut down on her parties or Martin could sell his whirlpool bath. But the real problem area would seem to be Martin's extravagant breakfast. We would advise he switches to a bowl of Honey Nut Loops instead.

Stealing your neighbour's light

Two basic methods:

1. Take a large parabolic reflector and affix to an outside wall of your house. Now carefully angle towards your neighbour's living room. Masquerading as a satellite dish the reflector will secretly beam back any light into your own home. And all for free.

2. Armed with a domestic Camcorder sneak into your neighbour's house and videotape one of his wall lamps onto an E180 cassette. On playback you will then have three hours of free lighting at the touch of a button (six hours if you have a long play recorder).

FUSES

Isn't it annoying when a fuse blows? But is it any wonder? In these cost-conscious times, cynical manufacturers are only too willing to make fuses out of cheap, thin wire which will immediately 'blow' at the slightest surge in current.

However, the BIYer need not be a victim of this shoddy workmanship. Dispense with the normal fuses in your fuse box and replace them with old-fashioned, hard-wearing 6-inch nails. Now nothing short of a direct lightning strike will stop your appliances from operating.

REWIRING YOUR HOUSE

If you live in an older-style property, chances are that rodents will have gnawed away at your wiring over the years leaving you exposed to all sorts of potential problems. It is a good idea, then, to think about rewiring.

This needn't be a daunting task. Taking a length of thickish cable connect one end to your fuse box and start to thread the wires through any small gaps in your walls. You'll find a small crochet hook will help. To get the cable from say, a cellar to an attic, tie one end of the cable to a whaler's harpoon gun and fire across the roof. (If you have any problems in obtaining a gun, the Icelandic embassy in London should be able to put you in touch with a whaling fleet).

ALTERNATIVE SOURCES OF ENERGY

Pet power

If your children keep a pet gerbil it is an easy matter to turn its exercise wheel into a small electricity generator. Peddling at an average

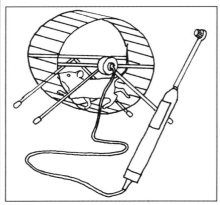

Make your Gerbil earn his keep

Using the power of the mind

In this New Age more and more people are discovering mind-expanding techniques that can tap the hidden powers of the brain and obtain power for free. Just look at some of the benefits:

- **Telekinesis — wheel your Hostess Trolley around your living room from the comfort of your armchair by the power of thought.**

- **Telephoto — take pictures of your family and workmates just by thinking about them.**

- **Telephonic — make phone calls without even lifting the receiver.**

- **Telescopic — see into your neighbour's front room without the use of binoculars.**

You may find that even after years of trying you will be unable to perform any of these tasks. Don't worry. In scientific terms you are Telepathetic.

speed of 4mph, a medium-sized gerbil can power a small domestic appliance such as a toothbrush for up to several weeks.

NOTE: When the gerbil gets tired simply replace with a fresh one.

Wind and solar power

In these environment-conscious times we should all be thinking about taking advantage of the free energy offered by the forces of nature. Wind and solar power are two examples of cheap, eco-friendly alternative power sources commonly available. However, as they require high gusts and constant sunshine in order to be effective, you will need to relocate to the middle of a desert.

Of course this might present one or two small problems. For example, you will face hideous temperatures, require several Hoovers to remove the sand from your carpets, be pestered by Bedouins offering to buy your wife, covered in camel spit and have to travel thousands of miles to the nearest Burger King. However any disadvantages will be far outweighed by the satisfaction of knowing that you have beaten the electricity board at their own game.

LIGHTING

Good lighting can really make a home. While a poorly lit room can

A poorly lit room

disguise any BIY blunders, it can also result in you and your family bumping into furniture and stepping on small household pets. So follow our easy guide and put a little light in your life!

Different types of lighting

• Arc lights — *for lighting your ark (see page 9)*

• Flood lights — *for lighting a flood (see page 9)*

• Spotlights — *ideal for highlighting objects. If you have an ageing aunt who spends her days sitting in exactly the same chair, why not make her a feature of your room by focusing a spotlight on her?*

• Ballroom mirrored globes — *reflect little mosaics of light all over the living room. Just rip up the carpet and slash your shirt to the waist for that authentic 'Come Dancing' atmosphere*

• UVB sunbed bulbs — *learn from Hollywood stars. Replace ordinary bulbs and walk around your house naked for an instant 'George Hamilton' look*

• Ambient lighting — *a simple red light bulb in a bedroom will create a warm and intimate atmosphere*

WARNING: Ambient lighting may attract undesirables such as Conservative ministers, judges and high church officials.

THE FULLY AUTOMATED HOUSE

For centuries it has been a dream. But today, thanks to leaps in micro-electronic technology, it's a reality. The fully automated house.
Just imagine the following scenario... You have brought a new 'acquaintance' home. As you walk through the door the sensuous strings of Mantovani start to purr through your porch and the coffee percolator automatically hisses into life. Stepping inside, a moving walkway sweeps you both off in the direction of the bedroom. At the foot of the bed, the covers magically roll back and a perfectly chilled 1985 Châteauneuf-du-Pape spurts out of a hidden panel in the bedside cabinet. Sounds incredible? Not any more. It's easily achievable — with a little BIY know-how!

To fully automate your home

You will need:
• *A 400 ram Sputnik II mainframe computer*
• *2,000 Duracell 'AA' batteries*
• *Several miles of cable*
• *A house*

First, set aside a small guest room. This will be the 'nerve centre' of your operation in which you must install your mainframe computer. You will also need a large pen or Dutch barn in your garden in which to graze the 400 rams necessary to run a powerful computer programme.
Now, connect a series of cables to every electrical household object following this simple circuit diagram:

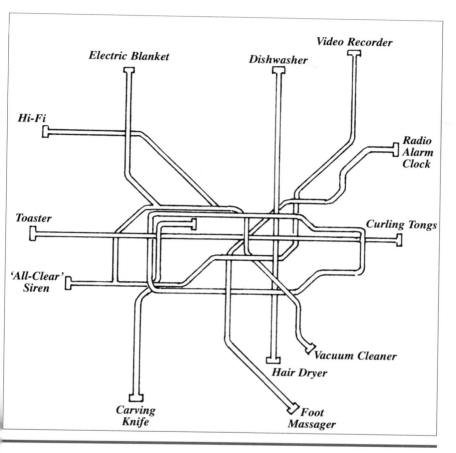

Video Recorder

Electric Blanket

Dishwasher

Hi-Fi

Radio
Alarm
Clock

Toaster

Curling Tongs

'All-Clear'
Siren

Vacuum Cleaner

Hair Dryer

Carving
Knife

Foot
Massager

TROUBLESHOOTING GUIDE

Problem: I have now put over 450 slices of bread in my pop-up toaster but not only have they failed to pop up, they've disappeared.

Solution: You are short-sighted and have posted your bread through the letter box.

Problem: My dishwasher smashes my crockery and worse, leaves items covered in a nasty grey slime.

Solution: You are extremely stupid and are putting your dishes into a cement mixer.

5
PLUMBING

Buried deep within your house is a complex labyrinth of pipes and ducts that is the very lifeblood of your home. Don't be daunted by this maze of metal. You may not know your ballcock from your U-bend, but even the most incompetent of BIYers can bodge their plumbing with absolutely no risk of turning their home into an Olympic swimming pool. Trust us.

Conventional plumbing relies on laying pipes in the most inaccessible parts of the home — under floors,

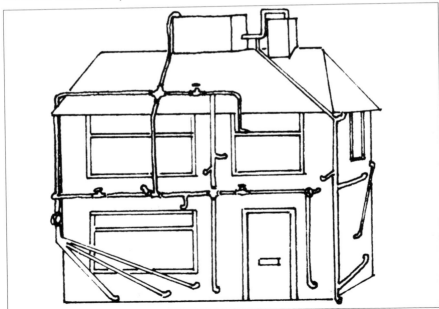

Pipes kept on the outside of the house are so much more accessible

between walls and rafters. This is tedious when they burst since you can't always get at them. Don't be caught out this way. Follow the example of top post-modernist architects like Richard 'Pompidou Centre' Rogers: stick the pipes on the outside of your house

To plumb your home

You will need:

- *A length of piping*
- *A deep sea diver's helmet*
- *Flippers*
- *A 25 yard swimming certificate*

PLUMBING TERMINOLOGY

Many terms associated with plumbing seem mystical to the layman. In reality though, they're very simple. Here's a quick guide:

- Bleeding radiators — a technical term used by plumbers when the little draining valve falls out of a radiator and a jet of filthy water spouts up the walls
- Bloody drains — another technical phrase, this time for when a drain is blocked with nasty little pieces of an indefinable brown squidgy substance
- Sodding sinks — an expletive

BURST PIPES

Every winter thousands of householders across the land are caught out by bursting pipes. Few household disasters can be so distressing; few can be avoided so easily.

To put an end to this annual misery simply place a couple of gallons of a proprietary anti-freeze in your main water tank.

Although highly toxic and likely to poison your entire family, anti-freeze is a good deal cheaper than calling out an emergency all-night plumber. Assuming that you can find one.

MENDING A LEAKING TAP

Drip, drip, drip. Drip, drip, drip. Drip, drip, dripperty drip. Drip, drip, dripperty drip drip… plink.

A dripping tap is enough to turn anyone barmy. And in many cases it does. History is replete with examples of lunatics who got that way because of a seemingly innocent little leak.

It is therefore vital that you always keep your taps in tip-top condition by regularly cleaning them with a pipe cleaner. However, if your tap does start to drip, get it before it gets you. While sticking a few tabs of Hubba Bubba bubble gum up the end may bring temporary relief, most people resort to replacing the tap washer. This can be a time-consuming and irksome task. Fortunately, there are excellent reasons why the BIYer should avoid it. Consider this:

It is a little-known fact that the world's washer supply is manufactured from a by-product of the near extinct Abyssinian Wottle Bird.

Cruelly plucked from its nest at just six weeks of age, the wretched creature is subjected to a life of misery in an overcrowded, airless pen. Bent double, shaking with fear, it is then taken away to be slaughtered before its beak is removed, ground down into a fine powder, mixed with

glue and stamped into the tap washers with which we are all familiar.

DO NOT SUPPORT THIS EVIL TRADE. BOYCOTT ALL WASHERS NOW!

Instead, should your tap develop a drip, save your sanity by abandoning the room and sealing it with one of those high pressure steel doors with a steering wheel stuck on it — like the ones used in old WW2 German U-boat movies.

UNBLOCKING SINKS

There is no need for using plungers or caustic soda whenever your sink becomes blocked; ultrasound waves will break down any impacted matter in the U-bend. Just hook up a

turntable by the sink and play old Bee Gees records.

ALTERNATIVES TO A WATER-BASED HEATING SYSTEM

Those clever old Romans certainly knew a thing or two about plumbing. Take a leaf out of their book by doing away with costly and inefficient water-filled radiators and installing underfloor central heating. Just follow our simple four-point plan:

1. *Rip up your floorboards*

2. *Light several small bonfires*

3. *Replace floorboards*

4. *Sit back and luxuriate in the gentle glow*

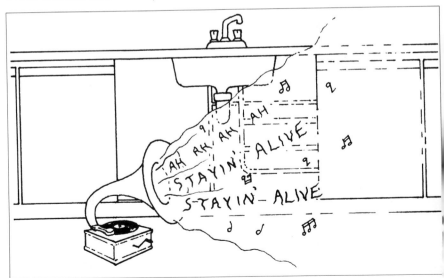

Unblocking sinks the easy way

A COMMON PLUMBING QUERY

Q. *I am a professional torturer and have always depended on old favourites like the red hot poker and the dripping tap. Admittedly these are a far cry from the state-of-the-art devices you see exhibited nowadays at the Teheran International Torture Show, but they have helped me secure a modest reputation in my field. My bosses are now insisting that I improve on my methods to get quicker results. Any ideas? (UVF, Belfast)*

A. *Ever since water was privatised, costs have spiralled. Now there's something actually worse than having 430 cubic litres of water gradually pounding a hole in your victim's head: facing the bill. Force them to watch the water meter relentlessly tick up the units while reading out a running total after every 20 drips.*

Remember, since hot air rises you'll feel more benefit the higher up you are. In this light you might like to move your children and ageing relatives into the chimney stack under the roof

MAXIMISING YOUR HEAT

People who live in large houses like the Queen often complain about taxes, cheap publishing scandals and the alarming divorce rate. But most of all, they moan about their heating bills. As a rule, the larger the house, the more expensive it is to heat. Having said this, even a small semi can throw up terrifying bills.

The answer is to minimise the space you need to heat. Make all your rooms as small as possible by constructing false interior walls.

Save heat with false walls

Insulating the whole house

Thinking on a larger scale, stop heat escaping from your home by weaving a 'house cosy' from old woollies.

TURNING YOUR HOT WATER SYSTEM INTO A TEASMAID

This is not such a crackpot idea as it may seem. By placing a few hundred tea bags in your main tank (the round ones with the little perforations work best) you will have tea 'on tap' around your home simply by bleeding the nearest radiator.

It's a good idea to keep a small jug of milk and a sugar bowl handy by each rad'

TAPPING INTO THE WATER TABLE

If you've ever been confronted with your water rates and thought: 'Jesus Christ!' why not consider an alternative? Obtain your own supply completely free by sinking a 150ft shaft into the water table using your pneumatic drill. The resulting geyser can be controlled with a large bung or stopper.

Where you suspect there may be acid rain contamination (such as next door to a nuclear reactor) strain the water through an old pair of tights. Add two Aspro Clear for extra safety.

FITTING A WASTE DISPOSAL UNIT

Although a good idea, in practice, fitting a waste disposal unit can be a tiring and dangerous job. Instead, if you're the owner of a Pit Bull Terrier or large Rottweiler, enlarge the plug hole of your sink using a 6-inch tungsten bit and install your dog underneath. Any scraps of food dropped into the sink will become an instant, nutritious meal for your pet. And your dog's growling will sound just like the real thing.

TURBOCHARGING A TOILET

Is your toilet slow to flush or prone to frequent blockages? Then it's worth considering turbocharging it to efficiently and speedily expel waste. This is easily achieved by fitting a standard 500cc outboard motor in the U-bend.

By connecting the motor's ignition pull-cord to the toilet chain the rotor blade will start to spin, breaking up stubborn waste matter the moment you are in flush mode.

MAKING BENDY TOYS FROM LEFT-OVER COPPER PIPING

While spending time bodging your home it's all too easy to forget about your children. They, after all, will be the bodgers of the future. So why not amuse them by making cute and cuddly toys from any odd lengths of copper piping you have left over after plumbing your house.

Using the Japanese art of 'Flexsushi' you can easily bend the pipes into charming animals.

Filled with boiling oil these loveable bendy toys also make unusual – and useful – bedwarmers for elderly relatives

GAS

Testing for leaks

In times gone by Welsh miners tested for escaping gas by employing a canary in a cage. Fortunately times change and so does technology. Today you can use a common or garden household budgerigar instead. Simply place the bird in a small cage as in *Fig a* below. If there is gas escaping the bird will assume the position as illustrated in *Fig b*.

Fig a

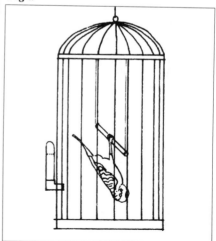

Fig b

SEEKING PROFESSIONAL HELP

There will be times when you have no alternative but to call on the services of a fully qualified gasman. When he arrives and looks at your installation you will be required to play your part in the following scenario:

Gas Man:
Is this 45 Acacia Gardens?

You:
Er... yes. Took your time didn't you? Why weren't you here six hours ago? I've had to take the entire day off work because you couldn't give me an exact time when you'd call

GM:
I don't make the rules, guv. Any chance of a cuppa?

You:
Er... Okay. But what about my leak?

GM:
(lighting cigarette) Yeah, alright. Let's 'ave a butchers.

A large, porky man stumbles into your living room leaving nasty footprints on your newly cleaned rug.

GM:
(sharp intake of breath followed by vigorous shaking of head) Oooh. No, no, no. Don't like the look of this. Don't like the look of this one little bit. Haven't seen one of those since 1947. What cowboy fitted this then?

You:
You did!

Gas man reaches for order book

You:
Well, can you fix it?

GM:
(another intake) Couldn't say. Depends.

You:
On what?

GM:
Parts, time, labour. Have to put in an order. Could take weeks...

You:
Weeks?

GM:
Months...

You:
Months?

GM:
Years. Taiwan, you see. You know what they're like.

Several months later one cold winter's day...

GM:
Morning!

You:
...pearing in sheepskin coat ...d fur muffler with chattering ...th and blue lips) ...nk God you've come!

GM:
...parky in 'ere, innit?

You:
...mmering with rage) Parky? ...ky? Of course it's soddin' ...ky. You've left me without ...gas for the last three ...nths!

GM:
...need for language like ...t.

You:
...ll, have you got it?

GM:
...t what?

You:
...know, the part!

GM:
...that. Nah. Sent us a ...V/406 by mistake didn't ...y. Lost the original docket. ...t's foreigners for yer...

You:
...oherent ravings)

Later still at the local gas showroom...

You:
...vsing yourself in four-star ...n a metal can) Excuse me. ...e you got a light?

Assistant:
No, sorry. You want the electricity showroom in the High Street.

You:
(with pained look of resignation) Oh...

Assistant:
But they're shut. Half day closing...

TROUBLESHOOTING GUIDE

Problem: I hear strange, yelping noises every time my washing machine enters the spin cycle

> **Solution:** Your wife is having sex with your next door neighbour, seeking to fool you by timing her moans of ecstasy with the whirrings of the machine. Contact a divorce attorney

Problem: It's like a sauna in here. The room is filled with dense clouds of steam and I'm sweating in temperatures of 120 degrees

> **Solution:** You are a Nubian masseur in a Turkish Bath suffering from short-term memory loss. Seek hypnotherapy

Problem: My water is coming out of my tap coloured brown with a curious white foam head

> **Solution:** Your malicious neighbour has connected his cappuccino maker to your water main. Connect your sewage waste pipe to his washing machine

6
HOME SECURITY

We live in violent times. In the few seconds it will take you to read this one paragraph, some 2,345 burglaries, 304 serious assaults and 23 murders will have been committed in Great Britain. And that could just be in your street.

We therefore make no apologies for dedicating a major chapter of this book to making your home a safer place for you and your family.

To understand how to go about installing the right security systems for your home, it is first essential to gain an insight into the workings of the criminal mind. In this light, we have interviewed Gerald (not his real name), a persistent offender currently serving 12 consecutive sentences for robbery with menaces.

> *I usually gain entry through a back window. You'd be surprised at the number of people who can't be bothered to lock them. Climbing up a drainpipe is easy. Then it's just a matter of heaving the window open and slipping in.*
>
> *First I go for the lingerie drawer in the bedroom. I love the feel of silk next to my bare skin, the soft caress of satin. Often I slip into a tiny pair of panties and gaze lovingly into a mirror, admiring the way that the material clings sensuously to my body. Sometimes I try on a bra. I like the ones that lift and separate, thrusting my chest into twin peaks of jutting perfection. Then I nick the telly.*

8 9 8 2 3 1

Posed by model

PREVENTION IS BETTER THAN CURE

Statistics show that most crimes against our property are committed by people we know. So it makes sense to take preventative steps.

Body-searching guests

Using an everyday Marigold washing-up glove (lightly lubricated with a squirt of Fairy Liquid) check that visitors to your home are not concealing any of your belongings about their person. You'd be surprised how easy it is for someone to hide a Wedgwood dinner service in their underwear.

Stickers

Crime prevention officers say that you should always aim to make your house more secure than your neighbour's. So use the special BIY cut-out sticker below.

Locks

Follow the example of your local bank and install time-delay devices to all your locks. Designed to open only for a few minutes every day these will baffle even the most determined villain. However, you will need to strictly regiment your lifestyle, as entry to each room in your house will only be possible for a few brief minutes in each 24 hours. It might be helpful to draw up a clock of room availability.

BODGE SPLODGE

f you are particularly poor at timekeeping, it would be wise to wire up a central klaxon to sound whenever a door is about to spring open or shut

Alarms

It's a world of bells, buzzers and beepers. How often have you been rudely woken by a car alarm at 2.00 am only to turn over and think,'Selfish sods. I hope they nick the bloody thing'. To prevent your home alarm having this effect on neighbours you'll have to try something different to get their attention.

We'd recommend connecting your

Burglars!

This house is BI-Wired for total security. However, my neighbour, Mr George Smedley of 43 Acacia Gardens, usually leaves his ground floor window open and has a rather nice canteen of solid silver cutlery in his living room sideboard.

alarm to a tape recorder and broadcasting an attention-grabbing message at 200 decibels. For example:

> 'Attention! Attention! You are invited round to number 45 Acacia Gardens where your neighbours, Ernie and Betty Bagshaw, are about to perform an unspeakably disgusting sex act with a root vegetable.'

Booby traps
Should your time locks and alarms fail, you will need a second line of defence. While the placing of mantraps, trip wires and anti-personnel mines around your home is an obvious precaution, it is essential to make a map of their location.

Digging a moat
Architects of Norman castles well understood the strategic value of a good, deep moat. Learn from history by digging a circular trench around your home and filling with undesirable and off-putting substances eg old toe nail clippings, bat guano, supermarket own-brand cola etc.

Closed circuit TV
Do you know who's on your lavatory when you're not? Ever wondered why your toilet paper so quickly becomes depleted? Install a closed circuit TV in your toilet and keep a watchful eye on what's going on. And who's going on it.

Other tips
• If you suspect the Milk Tray Man is parachuting in to visit your wife, trap him by sticking sheets of fly paper to the roof. Then taunt him with a stick

• Garden gnomes make handy

projectiles in the event of a break-in

• Do you own any valuable works of art? If so, disguise their true worth by scratching out tell-tale identifying signatures on the canvas:

• Etch your address on any other valuable objects you may own:

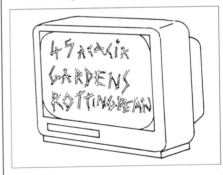

• If you have a young and vulnerable au pair you might like to consider drilling spyholes through your bathroom and spare bedroom walls. She will feel safe in the knowledge that someone is watching over her

• Keep small valuables in the hollowed-out pages of an old Melvyn Bragg novel or any other book

nobody would ever dream of reading

• Are you a wine buff with a cellar stocked with expensive vintages? Deter thieves by injecting the bottles with strychnine

• In the US there is a growing trend to steal not only the contents of a house but the entire house itself. Imagine going to bed in your suburban semi only to wake up on the back of an articulated lorry hurtling up the M1. Make sure this doesn't happen to you. Purchase an anchor from your local shipyard and fix to your house's foundations

DISSUADING RELIGIOUS CULTS

Scientologists, Moonies, Jehovah's Witnesses, Hare Krishnas, Born Again Christians. They're all out there.

Keep them out there by employing a few devious precautions. A couple of Aztec shrunken heads nailed over your front door should do the trick, however you might also consider painting a 12 foot pentangle on the roof or having sex in public with a dead chicken.

INTERROGATING INTRUDERS

These days, the police are far too busy catching people who have forgotten to return library books than to bother with someone robbing your house. So should you catch a thief in the act it will be up to you to disable him and keep him prisoner in an attic or cellar.

You will then need to mete out your own form of retribution. After all, if he is charged in court he'll only be sentenced to a two-month safari in Africa or at worst, a long weekend in

Centre Parcs.

Removing his eyebrows with a pair of blunt tweezers or sticking pieces of silver foil on his fillings is a good way to make him talk. Was he really after your video recorder? Or was he trying to steal your colour scheme?

Warding off delivery men

When is a milkman not a milkman? When he's a thief!

It's truly astounding the number of crooks who will pose as tradesmen to get into a house. It's therefore wise to ensure that delivery people have no excuse to come anywhere near your front door.
Try these tips:

● Drill a small hole in an outside wall and insert a thin plastic tube. Run one end to the foot of your front path and connect the other to a container in your fridge. Using a funnel your milkmen can pour milk straight into the kitchen without having to even set foot in the porch

● Place a ladder up to your chimney so that the coalman can empty his deliveries 'straight to the grate'

● Make a periscope from a cardboard tube and two small handbag mirrors to enable the gasman to read your meter from the garden fence

● Always give out your name and address in Serbo Croat to confuse postmen

NEIGHBOURHOOD WATCH

Recommended by police forces up and down the country, Neighbourhood Watch schemes have been proven to cut crime drastically. This is because they encourage people to scrutinise the behaviour of the very people most likely to commit crime: Their neighbours.

Take an interest in your community. Who is that busty blonde slipping into No 43 at 4.30pm? What is she concealing under her gold lamé basque? And why have the curtains just been drawn in the upstairs bedroom?

Keep a diary of your neighbour's movements, take photos with an infra-red night camera, place 'bugs' under his bed. Remember, once you have become an active participant of Neighbourhood Watch, it is your duty to be 'in the know'.

IF ALL ELSE FAILS...

Should you return home to find someone forcing your wife to do the washing-up at gunpoint you might like to consider becoming a vigilante.

To become a vigilante
You will need:
• A Magnum 44 revolver
• Several rounds of ammunition
• A copy of 'Michael Winner: My Life in Films'

Ask yourself: Who is this woman and what is she doing at No 43?

A COMMON HOME SECURITY QUERY

Q. *I live in a particularly rough part of Virginia Water and am anxious about going away on holiday for fear of burglary. I have fixed Chubb locks on all the exterior doors and security bars over the windows, but is there anything else I can do? (Lady B of F, Virginia Water)*

A. *Yes. Why not disguise your house as a police station? Stick a blue lamp above your porch with a sign saying 'Police Station'. If you are leaving your car behind, paint stripes on the bodysides and stencil 'POLICE' on the roof. Or tape an episode of The Bill on an endless loop tape and leave it playing in your lounge. Muttered sentences containing words like 'Whisky, Alpha, Foxtrot, Tango', plus the sounds of police officers beating up innocent suspects, should ward off any potential scallywags.*

7
FIXTURES
AND FITTINGS

helves, mirrors, curtains, walls. It's the little things that make a house a home.

In this chapter we turn the spotlight on fixtures and fittings, how to knock them up, how to put them up and how to stop them falling down.

THE BEDROOM
Mirrors

Many couples find that the stresses and strains of modern living can take the passion out of their relationship. If this sounds like you, inject a little eroticism into your love life by fixing mirrors to your bedroom ceiling. Popular in Japanese Love Hotels, they can be easily attached using double-sided sticky tape.

Obese partner? Delude yourself that she is only half her size by turning your bedroom into a fairground Hall of Mirrors. Mirror tiles can be easily 'bent' using a household oxyacetylene torch

Beds

If you live in a studio flat or small dwelling and are short of space, you might like to consider constructing a fold-away bed. To go about this sculpt a 6 x 4 ft recess in the wall where the bed is to go using your pneumatic drill. Then affix high-powered steel springs onto the side of the bed and the wall.

To prevent the bed suddenly springing up in the night splattering you against the wall, always sleep with lead weights in the turn-ups of your pyjama bottoms

THE LOUNGE
Futons

Extremely popular with the 'Habitat Set' in the seventies, these practical and comfy sofa-beds are making something of a comeback. Unfortunately they can be pricey. You can easily make your own futon by sawing off the legs from a conventional sofabed and stuffing the mattress with bricks.

Curtains

Why go to the expense? Simply draw the design of your choice onto the walls adjoining your window, taking care to recreate the pleats. You have now 'drawn' the curtains. Though, of course, you will be unable to actually draw them.

Blinds

Although stylish, blinds can often be awkward and fiddly to put up with their complex system of cords and pulleys. For a similar — and cheaper — effect, draw thick lines around your light bulbs with a felt tip marker. When switched on, the shadows cast will fool your neighbours into thinking you have expensive Venetian blinds.

Creating excitement in your lounge

Remember the heady exhilaration you feel at the airport as you sit waiting to board your holiday plane? The frenzied clicking of the departure boards as passengers scuttle off to far-flung shores? The anticipation of roaring off in a mighty jet for a two week orgy of booze and sex in the sun?

Well, why not convert your sitting room into an airport departure lounge and relive the thrill of foreign travel every day of the week.

Start by assembling your chairs and sofas into neat, orderly rows. Then if you have a computer, programme it to flash up departure information with a jolly 'Bing Bong' noise.

To further authenticate the experience, invite friends to slob around on your floor while their little brats run amok spilling beakers of Ribena down the walls — thus replicating perfectly a typical summer scene at Gatwick.

THE HALL
Fitting a catflap

When it comes to catflaps the choice is endless. Unfortunately they all have one major drawback. While they allow your cat to enter and exit your home, they also invite your neighbour's pets to pop in and leave their little 'signatures' all over your carpets. It's always been a major problem. Until now.

Trust those inscrutable Japanese to come up with the answer. Electronics giants the Katsubushi Corporation of Hiroshohama have devised a state-of-the-art electronic catflap with a number of built-in, high security devices.

Shortly available in this country (licence pending), the 'FlippertyFlap' feline entry system features a triple

Flipperty Flap: Front view

tumbler reinforced steel lock with a digital keypad. To install the assembly cut a panel in your door using the template provided. Now simply teach your cat to punch in the twelve digit combination necessary to open the flap. Katsubushi have thoughtfully provided handy 'paw-shaped' buttons to assist. Should another cat try to gain entry by tapping in an incorrect code, the flap will spring open and the luckless creature will get more than it bargained for.

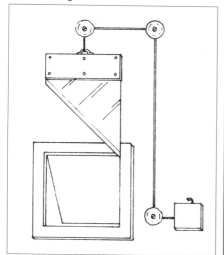

Flipperty Flap: Rear view

THE KITCHEN
Making sensible use of space

How often have you walked into someone's kitchen and thought: 'Blimey. There isn't room in here to swing a cat'.

Ensure nobody makes this judgement on your kitchen by sensibly planning its layout on paper before building starts.

Once work's completed, you will want to check that you have made optimum use of your space. Of course, we wouldn't for one moment recommend that you do this by actually swinging your own cat around. Instead, take your neighbour's cat, and hold firmly by the tail. Now hurl it round over your head taking care not to let it slip out of your hand. If the cat misses the walls by a whisker, your layout is ideal.

The working kitchen

Statistics show that on average, we spend over 15.75 years of our lives in the kitchen. In view of this you will not only want to create a practical and welcoming environment; you might also like to turn the time you spend there to your financial advantage.

To turn your kitchen into a drive-thru Chinese takeaway

You will need:
* *A large sledgehammer (to make a serving hatch)*
* *A copy of yesterday's Daily Star displayed on the counter permanently open at page 3*
* *10 tins of lychees, neatly stacked into a pyramid*
* *A calendar with a picture of a junk*
* *A TV tuned to MTV*
* *A wok*
* *A kitchen*

If you have no knowledge of Chinese cookery, don't worry. Here's a recipe to get you started:

To cook special fried rice
(to serve 250 people)
You will need:
- *375 cups boiled rice*
- *4 lts groundnut oil*
- *250 finely chopped spring onions*
- *125 lightly beaten eggs*
- *500 tsp thick soy sauce*
- *35 lbs pork bellies, roughly diced*

SHELVES

Putting up shelves is probably one of the easiest and most satisfying tasks the BIYer can undertake. Yet it can also be one of the most frustrating.

The problem lies not so much with the Bodger as the traditional spirit level used to get the shelves straight. Inherent design faults mean that the little bubble always irritatingly moves around.

But not with the Bodge It Level. Its unique, advanced design renders the bubble immobile thereby saving you hours of frustration trying to get it in the middle. Now your shelves will always be straight no matter what angle they may be!

bodge it level

BODGE SPLODGE Don't forget to screw the shelf assembly to the brackets on the wall. Otherwise, thoughtlessly placing heavy volumes at one end could catapult your Barbara Cartland paperbacks out of the window causing permanent brain damage to anyone passing below

SELF-ASSEMBLY FURNITURE

When purchasing an item of flat-packed furniture manufactured from Scandinavian pine, its assembly instructions will invariably be in Swedish. As this is a notoriously difficult language to master, opposite is a quick glossary of some of the more common phrases you might encounter when assembling a standard wardrobe.

What to do with the bits left over from self-assembly furniture kits?

Having assembled your kit you will now have a beautifully crafted piece of furniture. But what do you do with the numerous pieces of chipboard and odd-shaped clips that you will undoubtedly have left over?

The famous artist Picasso found the answer to this question. He created fine objets d'art from them. His 1926 sculpture 'Virgin on the Rocks' for instance, now hailed as a contemporary masterpiece and on display in the Googleheimer Gallery

Swedish

Visst är här många delar?

Benny, du vet den där skäggige i Abba... han klarade en gång en sån här

Det varade i alla fall inte så länge

Körde över den med sin Volvo

Har du kommit underfund med vilken som är den viktigaste biten än?

Den del utan vilken alltsammans brakar ihop

Hoppsan, den glömde vi att skicka med

Blimey, den här kartongen ser jättekonstig ut

Vänta lite, det är grejen du hanger tofflorna på

Jag slår vad om att du hellre skulle vara i bastun med Helga

...slå varandra med björkris och rulla nakna i snön på bergssluttningarna

Jag skulle inte varit en sådan snåljåp utan köpt färdigmonterat

English

Lots of bits, aren't there?

Benny, you know the bearded one from Abba... he made one of these once

Didn't last long though

Ran over it in his Volvo

So, have you worked out which is the most crucial part of the assembly yet?

The one without which the whole thing will collapse

Well, we forgot to include it

Blimey. This is a funny looking bit of packaging

Hang on. It's the thing you stick your slippers on

Bet you wish you were down the sauna with Helga instead...

... beating each other with birch twigs and frolicking naked in the cool mountain snow

Shouldn't have been such a mean old git and gone for the ready-made one in Minsk, was, in fact, made from two spare planks and a wire spring from an Ikea 'Snogg' sofabed.

SELLING YOUR PROPERTY

In today's cut-throat housing market you need to be one up on your neighbour if you are to sell your property. Here are a few suggestions on how to make your house that bit more appealing to potential buyers.

Blue plaques

People are more likely to view your property if they think that someone famous once lived there. So it would be to your advantage to stick a blue plaque on the front wall.

If you sense that potential purchasers may be sceptical, add a touch of authenticity by placing spent cans of hair spray and old stilettoes around the bedroom.

Decor

Every few years sees a new trend in interior decor. Last year it was the Renaissance Theme with winged cherubs and astrological symbols adorning suburban walls. But what next? Buyers are likely to be impressed if they think that they are moving into a 'house of the moment'.

Well, French design guru André Crouton has firmly predicted the answer. At the Maison Parfaite Exhibition in Paris he announced that the next major European decorating theme will be the 'Mediaeval Look'.

To achieve this, you will need to half-timber your lounge with fake oak beams and rip out the plumbing. You can pour the contents of your chamber pot into a central gutter or throw it out of a window. And if you have a particularly grotesque member of the family make gargoyles by waiting until he's asleep, then pouring molten latex over his face. A couple of black plastic rats will complete the overall effect.

Disguising bad smells

It's an old trick, but freshly brewed coffee and home-baked bread will disguise any lingering odours around the house eg a dead dog under the sink (see Plumbing page 36)

Local amenities

Easy access to public transport is a priority to many buyers, as is a friendly local pub. If you live in the middle of a Yorkshire bog with only half a dozen sheep for company this needn't be a problem. You can convince buyers that you live at the very hub of city life by making a bus stop sign from an old estate agent's board and placing it directly outside your house. Then pay friends to spend the evening staggering drunkenly up and down the bleak moorland wastes.

8
EXTERIOR WORK

ROOFING
'Above all a good roof'

It's an old maxim but one that holds as true today as when it was first penned by Michelangelo in 1542.

It is impossible to spend too much time, effort and money on insuring that your roof is kept in pristine condition at all times. You will need therefore to carry out regular checks by climbing to the apex.

Before you go it is essential to tell your wife and neighbours your itinerary, which face you intend to scale and how long you expect it to take. We'd recommend you allow about 4 days for the average Victorian semi.

To make the ascent

You will need:
- *Crampons, rope, bivouac*
- *A few volunteers from your local cub pack (to act as Sherpas)*
- *Union Jack*
- *Kendal mint cake*

Establishing your base camp above the porch, send one of your cubs up to the first floor window sill to calculate the best path to the top. If he fails to return or if you hear terrifying screams you can assume either that (a) he has fallen off the ledge or (b) he has encountered Yeti. Send up another cub. When you are sure that the route is safe, lasso your rope to a chimney pot and strike out to the summit.

Hurricane

If your roof blows away in a storm, your local BIY superstore can supply you with a new, ready-made one.

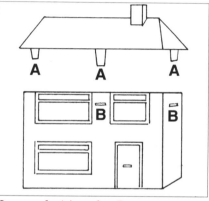

Locate tabs A into slots B

Nesting wildlife

A thatched roof is an ideal nesting site for all manner of wild creatures. Although at first this may seem appealing, you will not be laughing when a 60lb emu egg crashes through your ceiling. To lure out these pests you will first need to identify the type of animal residing in your roof to decide on the best method of eradication eg gun, gas or napalm.

Since you will rarely see these unwanted lodgers, here is a quick guide to tracks left by the more common species:

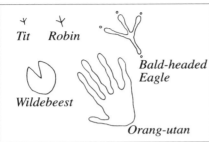

Tit   Robin

Bald-headed Eagle

Wildebeest

Orang-utan

Aircraft crash landing

As air traffic increases over our towns and cities, waking to find the nose cone of a 747 wedged in your attic will become more and more of a problem.

Should you find yourself facing this predicament, first pull the survivors from the wreckage and then go round and ask if they would prefer tea or coffee in a monotonous nasal whine. You might like to invite first class passengers into your lounge. These will be the ones stumbling around the fuselage in comfy slipperettes and eyeshades.

Once the crash investigation people remove the wreckage from your roof you can easily seal any hole with a small mastic gun.

Should you come across the black box flight recorder you'll find that it makes a super little pouffe for the lounge

GUTTERING

Gutters are designed for the efficient collection and disposal of rainwater. However they are prone to becoming blocked with leaves and other matter. Get round this problem by drilling large holes in them at regular intervals.

DOUBLE GLAZING

This is the one area the Bodger most definitely should not tackle. Fitting double glazing is a highly skilled job best left to the professionals. We'd recommend that you choose a glazing company such as our totally independent advertiser on page 54, with whom we have no connection whatsoever and from whom we have not — repeat not — received any inducements, financial or otherwise, to extol the virtues of their simply magnificent products.

FENCING

If horticulture isn't your forte you will find that in time, your garden will fill with a dense canopy of trees and shrubs, cutting out all sunlight and leaving little room for you and your family. To create more space, each night move your fence one millimetre towards your neighbour. This might seen a negligible distance but little by little, you will soon acquire more territory — as our chart shows.

Progress rate of territorial expansion by acquiring your neighbour's garden @ 1mm per day	
1 day	1mm
10 days	1cm
1 month	3cm
6 months	18cm
I year	36.5cm
5 years	182.5cm (6ft)
10 years	365cm (12ft)
20 years	730cm (24ft)

Thus in only 20 years you could increase the width of your garden by 8yds — that's almost the length of a double decker bus. And here's the beauty of the whole thing. Because you have moved the fence gradually, no one will ever suspect a thing.

CRAZY PAVING

As the name implies, only certified lunatics know the secret of laying this ever-popular stone surface. Under the government's 'Care in the Community' scheme you should easily be able to find half a dozen crazies wandering your neighbourhood. Equipped with pickaxes, mallets and a pile of rubble they'll make short work of the job. And possibly you.

PROBLEM AREAS

Woodworm

Considering the size of the average woodworm, its destructive power is truly awesome. Left untreated, an infestation can work its way through an entire house, reducing floorboards, furniture and timber supports to sawdust in a matter of seconds.

Until recently it was thought that woodworm were nothing more than primitive insect larvae. However, research by the von Haffenhöffer institute in Paraguay has shown this to be far from the case. Woodworm are, in fact, highly intelligent territorial predators closely related to the dolphin. To eradicate them from your home will therefore require psychological warfare and cunning.

To destroy woodworm

You will need:
* *A Cadbury's Curly Wurly*
* *A powerful electron microscope*
* *Some woodworm*

Place the Curly Wurly close to the area where you suspect the woodworm may be in hiding. Next, set up your electron microscope and wait. Sensing the presence of the chewy chocolate confection with their built-in 'radar', the creatures will slowly crawl out of the wood to feed. Von Haffenhöffer postulated that this usually occurred after an average of 3 hours 25 minutes and 15 seconds.

Now, keeping the vermin in sight through the microscope, whack the little bastards to death with a mallet.

Dry rot

Quite frankly the authors of this book are mystified as to why dry rot causes so many problems to so many people when it is so easily prevented. Simply hosing 20 gallons of water into the foundations of your house each morning and night will rid you of this scourge.

Rising damp

No one really understands what causes rising damp, least of all us. It probably has something to do with the position of the moon and planets. But we're not sure.

Fortunately we are sure of an effective way of eradicating the problem from your house: by introducing an impervious layer into your brickwork. The pros call it a damp course.

Start by hacking out a layer of mortar from your brickwork to a depth of 8.5mm (that's about 7.4 inches 'in old money'). Now slide several dozen panty liners into the resulting gap. We'd recommend the ones with little wings advertised by Claire Rayner. Your house will now be fully protected against damp.

GLAZIN ™

double glazing that's taken America by storm!

Thanks to revolutionary experiments conducted at zero gravity in the Kir Royale Soviet space station, we bring you an advanced new range of eco-friendly glazing that will add $$$ to the value of your home!

- ❏ *Made from 100% recycled cardboard*
- ❏ *Completely bullet-proof*
- ❏ *Fully transparent*
- ❏ *One size fits all*

Just look at what some of our satisfied customers have to say:

GLASS, CLEARLY A BETTER DEAL!

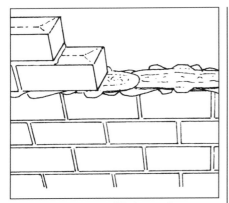

Panty liners can readily be used to create an efficient damp course

DEMOLITION
Walls

It's all too tempting to assume that a few stout blows from a sledgehammer will rid you of that tiresome and intrusive partition wall. Before embarking on such a project however, ask yourself the following questions:

a) Is it a load-bearing wall?
b) Could there be archaeological treasures preserved within?
c) Can my Vax 'Wet 'n' Dry' cope with sucking up 4 tons of rubble?

If the answer to any of these is yes — or even no — you must proceed with caution. Armed with a small teaspoon and a Swiss army knife carefully dismember the wall, piece by piece, taking care to number every section. With the help of an Arts Council grant you will then be able to reassemble the entire edifice as a thought-provoking exhibit in the Tate.

Houses

'No matter what I do to my home, I can never quite achieve the look I'm after'.

Sounds like you? Well, don't despair. Sometimes no matter how many walls we knock down or replace we are never going to be happy. Fortunately there is a simple solution.

To demolish your home

You will need:
* *One of those whopping great metal balls on the end of a chain*
* *A house*

A COMMON BUILDING QUERY

Q. I live in a tunnel complex in the notorious Iron Triangle area just north of Ho Chi Minh City. To be honest it's hardly all mod cons here — the roof leaks, you get earth in your Y-fronts and there are always weevils in the prawnballs. But, hey, we get by.

The main problem though are the people in the tunnel next door. They're up all night blasting out Jim Reeves records and playing Russian Roulette. It's driving me up the wall. We would get double glazing but we don't have any windows. Any ideas? (V.C., South Vietnam)

A. *Well actually you may be surprised to hear that those trusty chaps at Amazin Glazin™ have a product that could be tailor-made for you! It's easily fitted to your hatches and provides instant noise insulation. Just ask for VietCon™ Tunnel Glazing.*

9
BIY PROJECTS

N ow that you have a basic grounding in BIY techniques you will almost certainly wish to branch out on more ambitious schemes. After consultation with householders up and down Britain we have put together a list of the construction projects that met with most interest. We have rated them according to difficulty: the more splodges, the more tricky.

NUCLEAR DISPOSAL

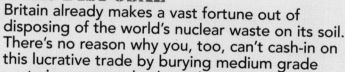

Britain already makes a vast fortune out of disposing of the world's nuclear waste on its soil. There's no reason why you, too, can't cash-in on this lucrative trade by burying medium grade nuclear waste in your own back garden.

Any number of foreign powers are begging to have spent nuclear fuel disposed of — and most will turn a blind eye to your qualifications if the price is right. So offer to remove it permanently for a modest fee — say fifty quid plus postage and packing. When it arrives simply dig a dirty great hole in the vegetable patch and turf it in. It really is money for old rope.

WARNING: *Burying nuclear waste in your garden may prove unpopular with narrow-minded neighbours. In this case it might be wise to change the name of your house eg from Sunnyview to Sellarscale.*

MAKING YOUR OWN SATELLITE RECEIVER

 The Internet, or Information Super Highway as it has been dubbed, is set to transform our lives. One day, in the not too distant future, we will all be able to fax, phone, watch television and order our pizzas at the press of a single button. News, views, gossip, information, all this and more will beam into our living rooms from around the globe.

Don't get left behind in this satellite stampede. Bodge a cheap and cheerful dish receiver from an old metal dustbin lid affixed to an outside wall.

WARNING: *You may find that using the lid from a rubbish bin results in your receiving poor quality television transmissions such as old reruns of Hart to Hart and Wonder Woman. This is called Sky One and is quite normal.*

INSTALLING A LIFT

Whether you share a house with an elderly amputee or you seem to spend your entire life running up and down the stairs, installing a lift is a good idea.

The first step is to bash a square hole through your house, from the upper floor down to the basement, using your pneumatic drill. Fitting four metal runners at each corner, install your lift, taking care to label the buttons correctly (see right). Hiring a bell hop to shout out the floor numbers will enable you to know where you are.

A quick floor guide

LEVEL 3
GRANNY FLAT
Wigs, corsets, prostheses, funeral services

LEVEL 2
KIDS' BEDROOMS
Dermatology, prophylactics, wines & spirits

LEVEL 1
WIFE'S BEDROOM
Perfumery, designer daywear, Italian leather goods

HUSBAND'S BEDROOM
Adult videos, binoculars, lingerie

GROUND
KITCHEN AND LOUNGE
Coffee shop, reception

LOWER GROUND
BARGAIN BASEMENT
Broken crockery, mismatched cutlery, old remnants, discontinued part-works, BIY

CONSTRUCTING A FAMILY CRYPT

Death.

Depressing, isn't it? But unfortunately a fact of life — albeit one we'd rather not dwell on. Still, the gloomy truth is that one day we'll all be dead. You, me, everybody. And we'll be dead for an awfully long time.

It makes sense then to start thinking about your demise now. After all, you wouldn't want to end up in a council plot with a cheap formica headstone, would you? Isn't it preferable to be buried with a monument that will honour your greatness for all time?

If so, you might like to consider constructing a family crypt — perhaps in the broom cupboard under the stairs. Although local councils tend to take a dim view of freelance tomb-building, you can get round their petty rules and regulations by issuing your own death certificates in illegible doctor's scrawl.

As each member of the family passes on, embalm the bodies immediately in Mr Sheen and wrap in old tea towels. You can knock up rough and ready coffins using chipboard left over from bodged shelving that's fallen off the wall.

As any Egyptologist will tell you, a good family vault should not only contain a priceless hoard of treasures belonging to the defunct occupants, it should also act as a time capsule telling future generations about the age in which they lived. You probably don't have a 24-carat gold funeral mask so how about one of those `My Little Pussy' collector's plates culled from a Sunday Express Magazine advertisement? A packet of Kellogg's Pop

Tarts? A set of lead crystal tumblers picked up for 12 Tiger Tokens? A gear knob from a Skoda Favorit?

After your demise, arrange with your neighbour to brick up the front of the crypt. As a final touch, a curse should be engraved on the door to deter grave robbers. Maybe something along the following lines:

> HEREIN LIETH THE MORTAL REMAINS OF THE LAST EARTHLY REPRESENTATIVE OF THE BAGSHAW DYNASTY. A POX ON HE WHO DISTURBETH THIS SACRED RESTING PLACE. MAY HE SPEND ETERNITY BROKEN DOWN IN THE CONTRAFLOW OF THE M25 BETWEEN JUNCTIONS 10 AND 11 WAITING FOR THE FREE RECOVERY SERVICE THAT COMETH NOT AND SUFFERING THE ABUSE AND VITRIOL OF OTHER IRATE DRIVERS STUCK BEHIND HIM IN THE PISSING RAIN.

CREATING A ROOF GARDEN

At best, living in the city can be exciting and stimulating. At worst, noisy, grimy, stressful. Surrounded by the ugliness and brutality of the urban environment, the human heart frequently longs for a haven of tranquil natural beauty.

A garden often fulfils this yearning. But if you live in a flat at the top of a house you might not have access to one. Still, all is not lost. You may create a rural idyll on the roof with a panoply of pots containing exotic flora. The advantages are manifold:

- **Sweeping panoramic views over the surrounding neighbourhood**
- **Fresher air**
- **Nude sunbathing away from prying eyes**
- **No doggy doo-doos**

The principal disadvantage however is one of gravity.

CRYOGENICS

Still on the subject of death, it's not all bad news. With a little enterprise you can turn it into profit by dabbling in the science of Cryogenics.

Put simply, Cryogenics is the art of preserving matter by means of deep freezing. It is particularly fashionable with Californians who are queuing up in their thousands to be frozen after death in the hope that medical science will one day come up with a cure for whatever provoked their demise.

TO TAKE UP CRYOGENICS
You will need:
• *A family-sized chest freezer*
• *A dead American*

It is desirable to store bodies intact. However, if freezer space is a problem, individual brains can be deep frozen in 'I Can't Believe It's Not Butter' tubs and stored in the ice box of your fridge.

As technology advances you can defrost your clients. Your average 240 lb Redneck obviously won't fit into a microwave, so do a deal with your local Trattoria to use their pizza oven.

BUILDING AN AQUATIC THEME PARK

Why pay well-earned money to visit an American-style amusement park only to be disappointed by the cheap and tawdry attractions when you can have a 'Never Never Land' in your very own back yard? Ever since audiences flocked to see Steven Spielberg's film 'Jaws', the lurking menace of the Great White Shark has entered the collective nightmare. Building an Aquatic Theme Park featuring these menacing man-eaters is therefore guaranteed to pull in paying visitors. If you have a small garden pond you're half way there. Simply...

PUBLISHER'S NOTE
The authors' manuscript ends here. Regrettably, before they could finish, they were admitted to a psychiatric unit for observation on medical advice. We are now given to understand that they are well on the road to recovery and plan to retire to a remote sharking station on a South Pacific atoll whence they hope to contribute a regular column to Fish Farming Today.

FIN